COOKING
THE
CUBAN
WAY

Lerner Publications Company
A division of Lerner Publishing Group
241 First Avenue North
Minneapolis, MN 55401 U.S.A.

Website address: www.lernerbooks.com

Library of Congress Cataloging-in-Publication Data

Behnke, Alison.
    Cooking the Cuban way : culturally authentic foods, including low-fat and vegetarian recipes / by Alison Behnke and Victor Manuel Valens.
      p.   cm. — (Easy menu ethnic cookbooks)
    Summary: An introduction to Cuban cooking featuring traditional recipes for yucca with garlic sauce, creole chicken, mango and papaya milkshake. Also includes information on the history, geography, customs, and people of this Caribbean island nation.
    ISBN: 0-8225-4129-7 (lib. bdg. : alk. paper)
    1. Cookery, Cuban—Juvenile literature. 2. Cuba—Social life and customs—Juvenile literature. 3. Low-fat diet—Recipes—Juvenile literature. 4. Vegetarian cookery—Juvenile literature. [1. Cookery, Cuban. 2. Cuba—Social life and customs.] I. Valens, Victor Manuel. II. Title. III. Series.
TX716.C8B44 2004
641.597291—dc22
                                    2003014496

easy menu ethnic cookbooks

COOKING

culturally authentic foods

THE

including low-fat and

CUBAN

vegetarian recipes

WAY

Alison Behnke and Victor Manuel Valens

⌊ Lerner Publications Company • Minneapolis

Contents

Introduction

The island nation of Cuba lies in the glittering waters of the Caribbean Sea, not far south of the United States. Havana, the capital of Cuba, is just ninety miles from Key West, Florida. Yet Cuba's culture is unique. Havana's broad squares, ornate fountains, and imposing government buildings have a European feel. Quiet fishing villages along the coast and homes painted pink, yellow, and blue evoke the colorful flair of the Caribbean. Cuba's Communist government has a tense relationship with the United States, but at the same time, vintage American cars roll through the streets, and most Cubans are enthusiastic baseball fans.

Cuba's history includes Spanish rule, slavery, and revolution. A vibrant, strong culture and an ethnically rich population have emerged. Musical traditions influenced by the original native inhabitants, by Spanish colonists (settlers), and by African slaves blended to create a uniquely Cuban beat. And culinary styles from many cultures come together in a cuisine that is as diverse as it is delicious. Hot white rice, hearty black beans, and the zesty flavors of tomato, onion, garlic, oregano, and cumin are the basic tools Cuban cooks use to create tasty, filling meals.

The rich flavor of garlic is abundant in both garlicky shrimp (top, recipe on page 50) and creole chicken (bottom, recipe on page 51).

The Land and the People

Cuba's territory covers fewer than forty-three thousand square miles, but this small area is rich in natural splendor. Ever since the Italian explorer Christopher Columbus landed on Cuba in 1492 and was struck by its lushness, visitors have been enchanted by the island's landscape. From the sparkling coastal waters to the dense, misty rain forests, the island is a Caribbean treasure chest of beauty.

Cuba's climate is warm for most of the year, although temperatures can dip into chilly ranges during the winter. The winter months are the driest, while a rainy season falls between May and October. The warm weather and plentiful rainfall have always been good for Cuban farmers. In the early years of Cuba's settlement, the island's rich soil nurtured crops such as corn, beans, yucca (a starchy root vegetable), squash, and peanuts. Later, the tropical climate proved perfect for growing valuable crops such as sugarcane, coffee, and tobacco. All of these crops remain important agricultural goods in Cuba, along with citrus fruit, rice, and potatoes.

The balmy, wet climate also allows rain forests to flourish in the southeastern part of the island. These lush areas are found on the lower elevations of mountain ranges, including the Sierra Maestra range. Its peaks jut out of the southeastern coast and slope down to the country's interior plains. Other mountains stretch across western and central Cuba.

Cuba's varied landscape supports a wide range of plants and animals. Mangrove trees thrive along the marshy shorelines, while hardwood trees such as mahogany and cedar grow in the island's interior. The massive ceiba tree, which can reach more than one hundred feet tall, was considered sacred by the island's first inhabitants and is still treasured by modern Cubans. A variety of flowers in vivid hues brighten the island's forests and fields. The white mariposa, a type of lily, is the national flower. Many colorful tropical birds also thrive on the island. The tocororo, the national bird, has red, white, and blue feathers—the colors of the Cuban flag. Offshore, coral reefs in the Caribbean Sea are home to delicate marine life.

Cuba's cities also offer diversity and contrasts. In Havana large luxury hotels and flashy nightclubs welcome tourists, while narrow neighborhood streets lined with crumbling buildings are crowded with bicycles, groups of elderly people chatting, and children playing. Cuba's second-largest city, Santiago de Cuba, is a business center and home to a Carnaval festival that is one of the island's biggest. But most of Cuba's cities and towns are rural, and residents make their living by farming or fishing.

Cuba's people are as varied as its geography, reflecting many heritages, traditions, and lifestyles. The island's first inhabitants settled the island more than three thousand years ago. The largest of these native groups was the Taino. They lived in villages and farmed the land, in addition to hunting and fishing for food.

The next people to arrive in Cuba were Spanish colonists. Along with other Europeans, the Spanish were settling islands throughout the Caribbean in the early 1500s. Hoping to strike it rich, Spanish conquerors forced the native Cubans to dig and pan for gold. Although some native groups tried to resist, they were unable to fight the better-armed colonists. The quest for gold turned out to be fruitless, but the search took a heavy toll on the workers. The back-breaking labor, combined with new diseases brought by the Europeans, killed many of the native people. By the mid-1500s, only a few thousand of the Taino remained.

The Spanish turned their attention to sugarcane, tobacco, and cof-fee—crops that grow well in Cuba and could be sold in Europe at good prices. Soon plantations (large farms) dotted the island. With few native Cubans left to do the farming, the Spanish joined in the swiftly growing Atlantic slave trade of the early 1700s. Ships bearing slaves from Africa began stopping in Cuba, and thousands of Africans were enslaved in Cuba over the next one hundred years. Slavery was finally outlawed in Cuba in 1886.

By then, the Cuban people were struggling to throw off Spanish rule. A series of revolutions and wars followed, and by the early 1900s, the nation had won independence from Spain. However, poverty, corruption, and political unrest continued to trouble the island for many years.

In 1959 a young revolutionary named Fidel Castro led a group that seized power of the country. Castro's government, which still holds power, is Communist. Communism is a political and eco-nomic system based on the idea of sharing resources evenly among a nation's citizens. Health care and education improved on the island after Castro took over. But his government strictly controls many aspects of Cuban life. Newspapers and other publications can pub-lish only material that has been approved by the government. Democratic elections are not allowed. Businesses also are tightly

Harvesting sugarcane is tough work. These Cuban harvesters take a break in the field.

controlled. For example, although families are allowed to run private restaurants called *paladares,* the restaurants are supposed to have no more than twelve seats. They must serve traditional, simple Cuban food, rather than fancier, more expensive dishes.

Many Cubans, unhappy with Castro's government, have left Cuba and immigrated to the United States. Because it is illegal for Cuban citizens to leave the country, many escape illegally, risking harsh punishment if they are caught by Cuban authorities. Large Cuban American communities exist in Miami, Florida, and in New York City. By opening grocery stores and restaurants, Cuban Americans have introduced the food of their homeland to people in the United States. At the same time, the Cuban and American governments have loosened restrictions on travel to the island, and many tourists have come to the island to enjoy the culture and cuisine firsthand.

Cuba's history has given the small nation a very diverse population. Although most of the native islanders died from overwork and disease, some intermarried with Spanish colonists. The descendants of these marriages were called *mestizos*. Islanders who were born in Cuba but had fully Spanish heritage were called *criollos* (Creoles). Further intermarriage took place between freed African slaves and both the mestizos and the criollos. Later

The fruit of the yucca plant is a common ingredient in many Cuban dishes.

immigrants added even more to the island's ethnic mix. As a result, modern Cuba is a collage of international traditions and ancestries. This rich multicultural heritage can be seen in everything from Cuban music to Cuban meals.

The Food

Cuban cuisine, like Cuban culture, has been shaped by many influences. One of the most traditional Cuban dishes—*frijoles negros*, or black beans—was first prepared hundreds of years ago by the island's native inhabitants. Many other Cuban foods have European origins. When Spanish colonists arrived on the island in the 1500s, they continued to enjoy the familiar dishes of their homeland. Entrées such as paella, a saffron-flavored rice and seafood dish, reflect the island's Spanish heritage.

But many old Spanish recipes changed when families prepared them in Cuba. Colonial cooks adopted some of the native fruits and vegetables that had been part of native Cuban cooking for generations. For example, *buñuelos*—the classic New Year's fritters—were made with wheat flour back in Spain. In Cuba they are prepared with cassava flour made from locally grown yucca. And, for centuries, the island's coastal waters have provided Cuban cooks with fresh seafood.

When African slaves were brought to Cuba in the 1700s, they, too, introduced their own cooking styles and dishes to local cuisine. *Tostones*, crispy fried plantains, are a traditional snack or side dish in many of the parts of Africa that supplied slaves to the Americas. In the 1800s, as the slave trade declined, laborers from China and other nations came to work in Cuba's sugarcane and tobacco fields. Over the years, many other immigrants from around the world came to Cuba, bringing their favorite recipes with them.

But Cuban cooking remains simple. Fresh produce and staples such as rice and beans are combined with a few key ingredients such as olive oil, garlic, oregano, and cumin. A sautéed mixture called a sofrito—consisting of garlic, onions, bell peppers, tomatoes and, depending on the cook and the dish, a variety of other spices and ingredients—is the foundation of many Cuban dishes. For example, the sofrito is the heart of *ropa vieja*, a rich dish of shredded beef. The narrow strips of meat and vegetables in this dish give it its name—ropa vieja means "old clothes" in Spanish. Other dishes that start with a sofrito are *carne con papa*, a meat and potato stew, and *picadillo*, a simple but flavorful ground-beef hash.

Another basis of many meals is *adobo*, a marinade of garlic, lime juice, and cumin. Cuban cooks often use adobo to flavor meat, poultry, and seafood before cooking. These simple starting points result in the hearty, flavorful food that Cubans of all backgrounds love.

Holidays and Festivals

Cuba's original inhabitants followed an ancient religion that had many gods and goddesses and included practices such as fortune-telling and healing rituals. Most of these religious traditions disappeared after the arrival of the Spanish colonists. The Spaniards introduced Roman Catholicism, a form of Christianity still practiced by many modern Cubans. Other Cubans belong to different Christian groups, and a small Jewish community also exists.

When African slaves arrived on the island, they brought their own beliefs. Over time African spiritual customs blended with Catholicism to create new religious traditions. In modern Cuba, the most commonly practiced of these blends is *santería*. Santería is rooted in the culture of the Yoruba, an ethnic group in Nigeria. Many slaves in Cuba came from Nigeria, and Yoruba rituals and gods and goddesses intermixed with Catholic rituals. In santería, Yoruba spirits, called *orishas*, are often associated with Catholic saints. For example, one female figure represents both the Virgin of Charity, an important saint in Cuban Catholicism, and Ochun, the Yoruba goddess of love.

After Fidel Castro took power, the Communist government discouraged the practice of religion. Religious holidays were officially banned until the 1990s. However, many Cubans continued to worship and practice their faith in private, and in recent years, religious celebrations have become more open.

Christmas, on December 25, is an important holiday for Christian Cubans. Although many Christmas traditions began to fade when the holiday was banned, in recent years more and more people have been celebrating Christmas openly. Festive decorations such as Christmas trees and lights appear in many Cuban homes and shops in December. On Christmas Eve—called La Noche Buena, or "the good night" in Cuba—most families share a large holiday meal.

Many santeros (people who practice santería) make altars such as this one to honor the orishas, or spirits.

Young people in costumes celebrate Carnaval in Santiago de Cuba.

Relatives from far away try to be together for this special night. Typical Christmas Eve dishes in Cuba include *lechón asado* (a roast suckling pig), beans and rice, and yucca.

After dinner many Cubans attend midnight Mass (a Catholic church service). In Havana church bells peal at midnight to mark the beginning of Christmas Day. The day itself may be spent visiting friends and family, attending church services, and eating delicious leftovers from the night before. In Cuba, as in Spain, gifts are traditionally not exchanged until January 6. This day, known as Epiphany, celebrates the coming of the three wise men in the story of Christ's birth.

New Year's celebrations have not had the troubled history that religious holidays have had in Cuba, and New Year's Eve continues to be a very festive occasion. Friends and families gather for parties, and brilliant fireworks light up the night skies in many cities. At the stroke of midnight, Cubans take part in an old tradition of eating twelve grapes—one for each month of the year. Many people also get rid of the past year's worries by tossing a bucket of water into the street from a doorstep or balcony—often soaking passersby! Lechón asado is a traditional dish on New Year's Eve, just as it is on Christmas Eve, and apple cider is a popular holiday beverage.

Another big event on the Cuban calendar is the summer Carnaval in Santiago de Cuba. Towns and cities all across the island hold summer festivals. The largest celebration takes place in Santiago de Cuba during July. Parades, elaborate floats, music, and dancers in sparkling costumes fill the streets, and large crowds turn out to join in the fun. The modern Carnaval grew out of celebrations held by African slaves at the end of the sugarcane harvest. African music and traditions—including some elements of santería—continue to play a role in the festivities. Hungry festivalgoers can satisfy their appetite with sweet or salty snacks sold by street vendors. Favorite snacks include tostones and buñuelos.

Like so much of Cuban culture, Cuban holidays have a rich history, filled with contrast and variety. But whatever the occasion, a Cuban celebration always brings together family, friends, fun, and food.

Before You Begin

Cuban cooking makes use of some ingredients that you may not know. Sometimes special cookware is used too, although the recipes in this book can easily be prepared with ordinary utensils and pans.

The most important thing you need to know before you start is how to be a careful cook. On the following page, you'll find a few rules that will make your cooking experience safe, fun, and easy. Next, take a look at the "dictionary" of utensils, terms, and special ingredients. You may also want to read the list of tips on preparing healthy, low-fat meals.

When you've picked out a recipe to try, read through it from beginning to end. Then you are ready to shop for ingredients and to organize the cookware you will need. Once you have assembled everything, you're ready to begin cooking.

Roast pork (recipe on page 64) is a tasty alternative to serving a whole roast suckling pig on Christmas Eve.

The Careful Cook

Whenever you cook, there are certain safety rules you must always keep in mind. Even experienced cooks follow these rules when they are in the kitchen.

- Always wash your hands before handling food. Thoroughly wash all raw vegetables and fruits to remove dirt, chemicals, and insecticides. Wash uncooked poultry, fish, and meat under cold water.
- Use a cutting board when cutting up vegetables and fruits. Don't cut them up in your hand! And be sure to cut in a direction *away* from you and your fingers.
- Long hair or loose clothing can easily catch fire if brought near the burners of a stove. If you have long hair, tie it back before you start cooking.
- Turn all pot handles toward the back of the stove so that you will not catch your sleeves or jewelry on them. This is especially important when younger brothers and sisters are around. They could easily knock off a pot and get burned.
- Always use a pot holder to steady hot pots or to take pans out of the oven. Don't use a wet cloth on a hot pan because the steam it produces could burn you.
- Lift the lid of a steaming pot with the opening away from you so that you will not get burned.
- If you get burned, hold the burn under cold running water. Do not put grease or butter on it. Cold water helps to take the heat out, but grease or butter will only keep it in.
- If grease or cooking oil catches fire, throw baking soda or salt at the bottom of the flame to put it out. (Water will *not* put out a grease fire.) Call for help, and try to turn all the stove burners to "off."

Cooking Utensils

food processor—An electric appliance with a blade that revolves inside a container to chop, mix, or blend food

meat thermometer—A thermometer used to measure the temperature of cooking meat to make sure that it is done

mortar—A strong bowl used, with a pestle, to grind, crush, or mash spices and other foods

pestle—A club-shaped utensil used with a mortar to grind, crush, or mash spices or other foods

ramekin—A small, shallow baking dish for making individual portions

spatula—A flat, thin utensil used to lift, toss, turn, or scoop up food

strainer—A bowl-shaped utensil used to drain or rinse food

whisk—A wire utensil used for beating food by hand

wire rack—An open wire stand on which hot food is cooled

Cooking Terms

baste—To pour, spoon, squirt, or brush liquid over food as it roasts or bakes in order to flavor and moisten it

beat—To stir rapidly in a circular motion

boil—To heat a liquid over high heat until bubbles form and rise rapidly to the surface

brown—To cook food quickly over high heat so that the surface turns an even brown

cream—To beat two or more ingredients (such as butter and sugar) together until the mixture has a creamy consistency

cube—To cut food into cube-shaped pieces

dice—To chop food into small, square pieces

grate—To cut food into tiny pieces by rubbing it against a grater

mince—To chop food into very fine pieces

pinch—A very small amount, usually what you can pick up between your thumb and first finger

preheat—To allow an oven to warm up to a certain temperature before putting food in it

sauté—To fry quickly over high heat in oil or fat, stirring or turning the food to prevent burning

seed—To remove seeds from a food

simmer—To cook over low heat in liquid kept just below its boiling point. Bubbles may occasionally rise to the surface.

Special Ingredients

bay leaves—The dried leaves of the bay (also called laurel) tree

capers—The small buds of a shrub that grows in the Mediterranean region and in Asia. The Spanish first brought capers to Cuba. Capers are usually pickled in vinegar and sold in jars.

cassava flour—Flour made from the starchy root vegetable cassava, also called yucca

chorizo—Pork sausage. Cuban cooks use Spanish chorizo, which has a much milder flavor than spicy Mexican chorizo. Look for Spanish chorizo at Latin American grocery stores or specialty markets.

cilantro—The leaves of coriander, a sharp-flavored herb used as a seasoning and as a garnish

cinnamon—A spice made from the bark of a tree in the laurel family. Cinnamon is available ground or in sticks.

cumin—The seeds of an herb in the parsley family, used in cooking to give food a slightly peppery flavor. Cumin seeds can be used whole or ground.

garlic—An herb that forms bulbs and whose distinctive flavor is used in many dishes. Each bulb can be broken up into several sections called cloves. Most recipes use only one or two cloves. Before you chop a clove of garlic, remove the papery covering that surrounds it.

mango—A tropical fruit with sweet, juicy, yellow flesh

olive oil—An oil made by pressing olives. Olive oil was introduced to Cuba from Spain. It is used in cooking and for dressing salads.

oregano—The dried leaves, whole or ground, of a rich and fragrant herb that is used as a seasoning

papaya—A tropical fruit with bright orange flesh. Papayas have a strong flavor that is both sweet and tart.

parsley—A green, leafy herb used as a seasoning and as a garnish

plantain—A starchy fruit that resembles a banana but must be cooked before it is eaten

red wine vinegar—Vinegar made from red wine. Wine vinegars usually have a sharp, tangy taste, with a deep flavor.

saffron—A spice, made from part of a crocus flower, that has a strong flavor and adds a yellow color to foods. Saffron is available in threads or in a powdered form. Powdered saffron is less expensive and easier to use than saffron threads. If saffron is too expensive, Cuban cooks often use turmeric instead. Although the flavor is different, turmeric gives dishes the same bright yellow color that saffron does.

yucca—A root vegetable, similar to the potato. Also called cassava, yucca can be baked, mashed, or fried.

Healthy and Low-Fat Cooking Tips

Many modern cooks are concerned about preparing healthy, low-fat meals. Fortunately, there are simple ways to reduce the fat content of most dishes. Here are a few general tips for making adjustments to Cuban recipes. Throughout the book, you'll also find more specific suggestions—and don't worry, they'll still taste delicious!

Many Cuban recipes call for olive oil to sauté vegetables or other ingredients. Olive oil adds good flavor and is healthier for your heart than the fats in most other oils, butter, and margarine. However, you may still want to cut fat by reducing the amount of oil you use or substituting a low-fat or nonfat cooking spray for oil. It's also a good idea to use a nonstick pan if you decide to use less oil than the recipe calls for. When recipes call for deep-frying, you may want to experiment with baking the dish instead to reduce fat.

Cuban dishes often call for meat. Cutting meat out of a dish is a quick way to cut fat. But if you want to keep a source of protein in your dish, there are many low-fat options. Try buying extra-lean meats and trimming off as much fat as possible or replacing ground beef with ground turkey. To both reduce fat content and prepare a vegetarian meal, you can use a meatless ingredient such as tofu, tempeh, or mock duck. Since these substitutions do alter a dish's flavor, you may need to experiment a bit to decide if you like the change.

Dairy and egg products are common in Cuban desserts. An easy way to trim fat from a recipe is to use skim milk in place of whole or 2 percent milk. In recipes that call for sweetened condensed milk, you may want to try substituting low-fat or nonfat sweetened condensed milk. Eggs can be replaced with reduced-fat egg substitutes.

There are many ways to prepare authentic Cuban meals that are good for you and still taste great. As you become a more experienced cook, try experimenting with recipes and substitutions to find the methods that work best for you.

METRIC CONVERSIONS

Cooks in the United States measure both liquid and solid ingredients using standard containers based on the 8-ounce cup and the tablespoon. These measurements are based on volume, while the metric system of measurement is based on both weight (for solids) and volume (for liquids). To convert from U.S. fluid tablespoons, ounces, quarts, and so forth to metric liters is a straightforward conversion, using the chart below. However, since solids have different weights—one cup of rice does not weigh the same as one cup of grated cheese, for example—many cooks who use the metric system have kitchen scales to weigh different ingredients. The chart below will give you a good starting point for basic conversions to the metric system.

MASS (weight)

1 ounce (oz.)	=	28.0 grams (g)
8 ounces	=	227.0 grams
1 pound (lb.) or 16 ounces	=	0.45 kilograms (kg)
2.2 pounds	=	1.0 kilogram

LIQUID VOLUME

1 teaspoon (tsp.)	=	5.0 milliliters (ml)
1 tablespoon (tbsp.)	=	15.0 milliliters
1 fluid ounce (oz.)	=	30.0 milliliters
1 cup (c.)	=	240 milliliters
1 pint (pt.)	=	480 milliliters
1 quart (qt.)	=	0.95 liters (l)
1 gallon (gal.)	=	3.80 liters

LENGTH

¼ inch (in.)	=	0.6 centimeters (cm)
½ inch	=	1.25 centimeters
1 inch	=	2.5 centimeters

TEMPERATURE

212°F	=	100°C (boiling point of water)
225°F	=	110°C
250°F	=	120°C
275°F	=	135°C
300°F	=	150°C
325°F	=	160°C
350°F	=	180°C
375°F	=	190°C
400°F	=	200°C

(To convert temperature in Fahrenheit to Celsius, subtract 32 and multiply by .56)

PAN SIZES

8-inch cake pan	=	20 x 4-centimeter cake pan
9-inch cake pan	=	23 x 3.5-centimeter cake pan
11 x 7-inch baking pan	=	28 x 18-centimeter baking pan
13 x 9-inch baking pan	=	32.5 x 23-centimeter baking pan
9 x 5-inch loaf pan	=	23 x 13-centimeter loaf pan
2-quart casserole	=	2-liter casserole

A Cuban Table

Over the course of Cuba's history, many of its people have struggled with poverty. In some areas, the gap between the rich and the poor remains great. Despite this divide, one thing that all Cubans have in common is a love of food. No matter what kind of house the table is in or how fancy the silverware is, the black beans and rice are the same. Cuban families of all backgrounds enjoy traditional favorite dishes.

Of course, Cubans' eating habits do vary. Many farmworkers and others who do hard physical work eat large *desayunos* (breakfasts). But most of the island's residents start the day with a light meal of *café con leche* (strong coffee with milk) and bread with butter or olive oil.

Many Cubans come home for a midday meal (*almuerzo*) and a short rest, especially in summer's heat. Lunch may include salad, rice, and soup. Favorite beverages are *guarapo* (a refreshing sugarcane drink), a wide variety of other soft drinks, and juices.

Dinner (*cena*), usually eaten around 8:00 P.M., is leisurely. Diners often chat and sip coffee long after the meal is over. Cubans also love to snack, and an old standard is the *medianoche*. The name of this grilled meat and cheese sandwich means "midnight." Hungry locals eat medianoches at almost any time of the day.

Cuba is a small island with many influences. But from café con leche to medianoches, favorite foods link all Cubans together.

Mealtime is an excellent opportunity for Cubans to come together. Sidewalk cafés provide the perfect setting for a relaxed lunch or dinner.

A Cuban Menu

Below are suggested menus for two typical Cuban meals, along with shopping lists of the ingredients you'll need to prepare them. These are just a few possible combinations of dishes and flavors. As you gain more experience with Cuban cooking, you may enjoy designing your own menus and meal plans.

LUNCH

Avocado salad

Beef hash

Cuban white rice

SHOPPING LIST:

Produce

1 head lettuce
4 avocados
1 red onion
2 yellow onions
2 green bell peppers
1 bulb garlic

Dairy/Egg/Meat

1 lb. lean ground beef

Canned/Bottled/Boxed

16 oz. canned tomato sauce
1 small jar sliced green olives
    with pimientos
olive oil
red wine vinegar

Miscellaneous

medium- or long-grain white
    rice
golden raisins
cumin
oregano
salt
black pepper

SUPPER

Garlic soup

Creole chicken

Red beans and rice

Baked custard

SHOPPING LIST:

Produce

3 bulbs garlic
4 yellow onions
3 green bell peppers, or 2
   green peppers and 1 red
   bell pepper
fresh cilantro

Dairy/Egg/Meat

4 eggs
4 to 6 boneless, skinless
   chicken breasts (1 to 1½ lb.)

Canned/Bottled/Boxed

olive oil
32 oz. chicken broth
16 oz. canned tomato sauce
14-oz. can sweetened
   condensed milk
12-oz. can evaporated milk
red wine vinegar
1 small jar sliced green olives
   with pimientos
capers
vanilla extract

Miscellaneous

1 c. dried small red kidney
   beans
long-grain white rice
2 slices bread (stale or day-
   old, if possible)
raisins
cumin
oregano
bay leaves
sugar
salt
black pepper

Salads, Soups, and Stews

Classic Cuban meals center on robust meat dishes, along with starches such as rice, beans, and yucca. However, lighter fruit and vegetable salads also show up on Cuban tables. Basic green salads are standard in many homes, but unique combinations such as onion and pineapple also delight diners' taste buds. Avocado is a popular salad ingredient, and favorite fruits include mangoes and papayas. Heartier salads may call for ingredients such as beans or rice. Creamy chicken or fish salads are also popular, especially at parties and other social occasions.

Soups and stews are an important part of Cuban cooking as well. The midday meal often includes soup. Some Cuban soups, such as the beef stew called carne con papa, are filling enough to be main courses. During the hot summer months, some cooks like to serve refreshing chilled soups.

Avocado salad (top, recipe on page 34) is a colorful and nutritious addition to any meal. Serve it with garlic soup (bottom, recipe on page 35) for a light lunch.

Garbanzo Bean Salad / *Ensalada de Garbanzos*

Serve this chilled salad as a light lunch or as a satisfying starter for supper on a hot day.

2½ c. canned garbanzo beans*, rinsed and drained

1 green bell pepper, seeded and chopped

1 red bell pepper, seeded and chopped

1 red onion, chopped

Dressing:

3 tbsp. red wine vinegar

¼ c. olive oil

½ tsp. cumin

2 cloves garlic, peeled and minced

salt and pepper to taste

1. In a large bowl, combine garbanzo beans, green and red pepper, and onion.

2. In a small bowl, make dressing by whisking together vinegar, olive oil, cumin, garlic, salt, and pepper.

3. Pour dressing over garbanzo bean mixture and toss gently. Serve chilled.

Preparation time: 10 to 15 minutes (plus chilling time)
Serves 4

*If you prefer to use dried garbanzo beans, soak 1 lb. garbanzo beans overnight. Drain and add beans to 8 c. boiling water. Reduce heat, cover, and simmer with 1 tbsp. salt for 1 hour and 15 minutes, or until tender. Drain and proceed with Step 1.

Avocado Salad / Ensalada de Aguacate

This basic salad is a Cuban classic. For a colorful variation, add 2 c. of pineapple chunks.

4 to 6 large lettuce leaves, such as iceberg or romaine, rinsed and patted dry

4 medium avocados*

1 small red onion

Dressing:

2 to 3 tbsp. olive oil

3 tbsp. red wine vinegar

salt to taste

1. Spread lettuce leaves on a platter or large plate.

2. Peel avocados and slice into wedges. Arrange wedges on top of lettuce.

3. Peel onion and slice into thin rings. Place rings on top of avocado.

4. In a small bowl, make dressing by combining olive oil and vinegar. Sprinkle salad with salt, drizzle with olive oil mixture, and serve.

Preparation time: 15 to 20 minutes
Serves 4 to 6

Look for avocados that are slightly soft but not mushy. If avocados are too hard to use, let them sit on a shelf or countertop for a few days until they soften. To peel, carefully use a sharp knife to cut avocado in half lengthwise, cutting around the large pit. Gently twist the two halves apart and use your fingers or a spoon to remove and discard the pit. Place the halves cut side down and use a large serving spoon to scoop the avocado out of the skin, being careful not to mash the halves.

Garlic Soup / Sopa de Ajo

This simple but flavorful soup uses lots of garlic—a favorite ingredient in Cuban cooking.

2 tbsp. olive oil

6 cloves garlic, peeled and crushed*

2 slices stale bread, cubed

4 c. chicken broth**

I bay leaf

½ tsp. salt

I egg**

1. In a deep saucepan, heat oil over medium-high heat. Add crushed garlic and bread cubes. Sauté 2 to 3 minutes, or until garlic is golden but not burnt.

2. Remove bread and garlic to a small bowl. Using a fork or a wooden spoon, mash garlic and bread together. Return bread and garlic to saucepan and add chicken broth, bay leaf, and salt. Stir well. Turn heat to high and bring mixture to a boil. Then reduce heat and simmer for 5 minutes.

3. In a small bowl, beat egg well. Stir into soup and serve immediately, piping hot.

Preparation time: 5 to 10 minutes
Cooking time: 10 minutes
Serves 4

*To crush a clove of garlic, press the flat side of a knife against it. The clove will be flattened and slightly separated but should remain in one piece.

**To reduce the fat content of garlic soup and make it a vegetarian dish, substitute vegetable stock or water for the chicken broth and do not add the egg. If using water instead of broth, you may need to add more salt.

Meat and Potato Stew / *Carne con Papa*

This robust stew is a home-style favorite in Cuba. Served hot with crusty bread, it makes a satisfying dinner on a cool evening.

3 tbsp. olive oil

2 medium onions, chopped

1 large green bell pepper, seeded and chopped

3 cloves garlic, peeled and minced

2 bay leaves

1 15-oz. can tomato sauce

2 tbsp. red wine vinegar

1½ tbsp. capers

⅓ c. green olives with pimientos, cut in half

2 c. water

2 lb. boneless chuck steak, cut into 1-in. cubes*

6 to 8 medium-sized potatoes, peeled and cubed

salt to taste

1. Heat oil in a large stockpot over medium heat. Sauté onions and green pepper for 2 to 3 minutes, or until onions are soft but not brown.

2. Add garlic, bay leaves, tomato sauce, vinegar, capers, and olives and cook for about 5 minutes. (This onion-pepper mixture is the sofrito.)

3. Add water and meat to sofrito and cook 20 minutes. Finally, add potatoes, cover, and simmer 15 minutes, or until meat and potatoes are tender. Add salt to taste and serve hot.

Preparation time: 15 to 25 minutes
Cooking time: 45 minutes
Serves 6 to 8

*For a stew without the carne (meat), omit the steak and double the number of potatoes. You may also want to throw in some of your other favorite veggies, such as carrots, eggplant, or green beans.

Staples and Side Dishes

A few staples form the basis of Cuban cooking. These include creole sauce—a tomato sauce flavored with olive oil, garlic, and oregano—black beans, and white rice. A variety of side dishes usually round out meals of meat or fish. Filling, starch-based dishes are prepared with the island's native produce, such as yucca, plantains, and potatoes. Other delicious starchy vegetables, such as the yamlike root vegetables *malanga* and *boniato*, also add flavor and substance to Cuban meals.

Most Cuban side dishes can be eaten with any meal. In fact, various preparations of beans and rice, the most common side dishes, are present at nearly every meal—breakfast, lunch, and dinner. Served in larger portions, rice and beans and other side dishes can also make satisfying main courses. Try pairing a few of these tasty offerings with a salad or meatless soup to create a delicious vegetarian meal.

These crispy fried plantains (recipe on pages 46–47) are a tasty treat anytime, whether as a light snack, appetizer, or side dish.

Creole Sauce/ Salsa Criolla

This flavorful sauce is the foundation of many Cuban dishes. Spanish in origin, it is named for the criollos, or Cubans of European heritage. This recipe is the one used by author Victor Manuel Valens at his restaurant.

4 tbsp. olive oil

1 large yellow onion, sliced into narrow wedges

1 large green bell pepper, seeded and cut into ¼-inch-wide strips

6 to 8 cloves garlic, peeled and minced

2 c. tomato sauce

1 c. red wine vinegar

½ tsp. oregano

salt and pepper to taste

1. Heat oil in a large saucepan or skillet over medium-high heat. Add onion, green pepper, and garlic. Sauté 3 to 4 minutes, or until onion and green pepper are soft.

2. Add tomato sauce, vinegar, oregano, and salt and pepper. Reduce heat, cover, and simmer 10 to 15 minutes.*

Preparation time: 10 minutes
Cooking time: 15 to 20 minutes
Makes about 3 cups

Because creole sauce is used in so many recipes, you may want to make a batch and store it when you're planning to do some Cuban cooking. If the sauce is placed in a tightly sealed container and refrigerated, it will keep for five to seven days.

Cuban White Rice / *Arroz Blanco Cubano*

White rice is a Cuban staple, and it goes well with many entrées.

1½ c. long-grain white rice

1 tbsp. olive oil

1 clove garlic, peeled and crushed

2 c. water

½ tsp. salt

1. Put rice in a strainer and rinse in cold water until water runs almost clear.

2. In a large saucepan, heat oil over medium heat. Add garlic and sauté 2 minutes, or until garlic is brown but not burned. Use a slotted spoon to remove garlic and discard. (The garlic is used only to flavor the oil.)

3. Add rice to pan. Stir carefully to coat rice lightly with oil. Add water and salt and raise heat to high. Bring to a boil, return heat to medium-low, and cover pan. Simmer for 25 minutes, adding water if necessary, until rice is tender and fluffy.

Preparation time: 5 minutes
Cooking time: 35 minutes
Serves 4 to 6

Yellow Rice/Arroz Amarillo

Saffron gives this rice dish its color and its name. Yellow rice is often paired with black beans or chicken. Spanish chorizo, shrimp, pork, or other extra ingredients are often added to this dish for a flavorful treat.

2 tbsp. olive oil

1 small yellow onion, chopped

1 clove garlic, peeled and minced

1¼ c. water

1 c. chicken broth or vegetable stock

½ tsp. salt

⅛ tsp. powdered saffron, or ¾ tsp. turmeric

1 c. long-grain white rice

1. In a large saucepan, heat oil over medium heat and sauté onion and garlic 2 to 3 minutes, or until onion is soft but not brown.*

2. Add water, chicken broth or vegetable stock, salt, and saffron or turmeric to pan. Increase heat to medium-high and bring to a boil. Add rice and stir.

3. Cover pot, reduce heat to medium-low, and simmer 20 minutes, stirring occasionally. Remove from heat. Let stand for a few minutes, then fluff with a fork and serve.

Preparation time: 10 minutes
Cooking time: 30 to 40 minutes
Serves 4

*For an easy variation with a deeper color and extra flavor, skip to Step 2 and replace the oil, onion, garlic, water, and broth with 2 c. creole sauce (recipe on page 40). Simply boil the creole sauce, salt, and saffron together before adding the rice.

Black Beans/Frijoles Negros

Black beans are one of the most distinctively Cuban dishes. Filling, low fat, and delicious, they are frequently prepared as a side dish. Served with white rice (recipe on page 41), they also make a hearty main course.

1½ c. dried black beans

1 medium green bell pepper, cut in half and seeded

6 c. cold water

1 medium onion

3 cloves garlic, peeled

2 tsp. plus 1 tsp. salt

2 tbsp. olive oil

3 tbsp. sugar

2 tsp. ground cumin

1 tsp. oregano

1 bay leaf

1 tsp. black pepper

1 tbsp. white vinegar

1. Wash beans, removing any small stones or other debris. Place beans in a large pot or bowl with enough water to cover. Cut a 1-inch-wide strip of green pepper and add to the beans. Allow to soak 8 hours or overnight.*

2. Drain beans and place in a large pot with 6 c. water. Place pot over high heat and bring to a boil. Reduce heat to low, cover, and simmer.

3. Meanwhile, chop onion and remaining green pepper. Using a mortar and pestle or a small bowl and a fork or the back of a spoon, mash garlic with 2 tsp. salt.

4. Place oil in a skillet over medium heat. Add onion and green pepper and sauté for 1 minute. Add mashed garlic and salt and sauté 1 more minute, or until onions are soft but not brown.

5. Add onion mixture to beans. Add sugar, cumin, oregano, bay leaf, pepper, and the remaining salt. Stir well.

6. Continue simmering beans, stirring occasionally to prevent them from sticking to the bottom of the pan. Simmer for 1 hour and 15 minutes, or until liquid is mostly absorbed and beans are very tender. If the liquid is absorbed before the beans are done, add more water, ½ c. at a time.

7. A few minutes before beans are done, remove 1 c. beans from pot and mash with a fork until they have a pastelike consistency. Return to pot. Remove bay leaf and discard. Stir in vinegar and cook 5 minutes more. Add additional salt and pepper to taste, and serve hot with white rice.

*Preparation time: 15 to 20 minutes
(plus 8 hours soaking time)
Cooking time: 1½ to 2 hours
Serves 4 to 6*

**If you need to make black beans in a hurry, skip Steps 1 and 2
and replace the dried beans and water with two 15-oz. cans
black beans and their liquid. After sautéing onion, pepper, and
garlic, combine them with the beans in a stockpot or large, deep
skillet. Proceed with Step 5. Using canned beans, you will only
need to simmer the mixture for about 15 minutes in Step 6.*

Fried Plantains / Tostones

These crispy bites of plantain are special because they're fried twice. Look for plantains at your grocery store or supermarket. If you don't find them there, try an African or Latin American specialty market.

2 or 3 unripe (green) plantains

vegetable oil for frying

1 tbsp. salt

6 c. warm water

salt to taste

1. Peel the plantains and slice into 1- to 1½-inch rounds.*

2. Pour oil into a large, heavy skillet until the oil is about 1 inch deep. Heat oil over medium-high heat for 4 or 5 minutes. Carefully place plantain slices in oil and fry for 4 or 5 minutes on each side, or until they are beginning to turn golden.

3. Using a spatula, carefully remove plantains from oil and place on paper towels to drain. Remove skillet from heat.

4. In large bowl, combine salt and warm water and stir.

5. Place one plantain slice in a brown paper bag. Use the bottom of a cup to firmly press down on the slice until it is about half its original thickness. Remove slice from bag and place in the bowl of salt water. Repeat until all slices have been pressed.

6. Allow slices to soak in salt water for about 5 minutes longer. Remove and drain on paper towels.

7. Reheat the oil over medium heat. Fry slices a second time, for about 2 minutes on each side, or until they are warm and have turned a bit darker. Remove from oil and drain again on paper towels.

8. Sprinkle warm tostones with salt and serve immediately.

Preparation time: 20 minutes
Cooking time: 10 to 15 minutes
Serves 4 to 6

The best way to peel plantains varies, depending on how they are being used. For this dish, use a sharp knife to slit the peel lengthwise, from one end of the plantain to the other. Next, slice the plantain into rounds and use your fingers to peel each piece.

Main Dishes

Historically, the main dishes in Cuban meals have featured meat as the main ingredient. Pork is the most popular main course on the island. Chicken, beef, and seafood entrées are also common on local menus. Cuban cooks often use simple preparation techniques to make the most of flavorful, freshly caught seafood.

Despite the traditional focus on meat dishes, Cuban cuisine also offers tempting vegetarian courses. Dishes of rice and vegetables make good use of fresh produce. Many meat recipes can be adapted and served as part of vegetarian meals.

Most Cuban entrées can be eaten as part of any meal. Prepare these main dishes anytime to enjoy a delicious Cuban meal.

Pair baked eggs (bottom, recipe on page 55) with beef hash (top, recipe on page 54) for a hearty breakfast or lunch.

Garlicky Shrimp/ *Camarones al Ajillo*

Try serving this entrée with Cuban white rice (recipe on page 41) for an elegant Caribbean meal.

3 to 4 tbsp. olive oil

20 medium shrimp, peeled and
    deveined,* or 1 7-oz. package
    frozen raw shrimp, thawed

6 cloves garlic, peeled and sliced

juice of 1 medium lime (about 2 to
    3 tbsp.)

1 tsp. salt

1 tsp. black pepper

2 tbsp. chopped fresh parsley

1. In a large, heavy skillet, heat olive oil over medium heat. When you can smell the oil's aroma, or after 2 to 3 minutes, carefully add the shrimp and garlic.

2. Sauté shrimp and garlic for about 3 minutes, or until shrimp turns pink. Add lime juice, salt, and pepper. Cook for 2 minutes more.

3. Remove shrimp from pan and place on a serving dish. Spoon juices over shrimp and garnish with chopped parsley.

Preparation time: 5 to 10 minutes
Cooking time: 5 to 10 minutes
Serves 4

*Frozen shrimp usually come deveined. If you use fresh shrimp for this recipe, you may be able to have it peeled and deveined at the grocery store. Otherwise, you can do it yourself. Hold the shrimp so that the underside is facing you. Starting at the head, use your fingers to peel off the shell from the head toward the tail. Then, using a sharp knife, carefully make a shallow cut all the way down the center of the back. Hold the shrimp under cold running water to rinse out the dark vein.

Creole Chicken / *Pollo a la Criolla*

There are many versions of this classic Spanish-influenced dish. This one uses tender chicken breasts and is rich with the flavors of garlic and tomato.

4 tbsp. olive oil

4 to 6 boneless, skinless chicken breasts (1 to 1½ lb.), rinsed and patted dry*

2 c. creole sauce (recipe on page 40)

1 small green bell pepper, seeded and chopped

2 to 3 tbsp. each raisins, capers, and sliced green olives with pimientos to garnish (optional)

1. In a large skillet, heat oil over medium-high heat. Add chicken and cook 20 minutes, or until lightly browned, turning regularly to cook evenly.

2. Add creole sauce and green pepper to skillet. Lower heat, cover, and simmer 15 minutes more, or until chicken is done but not too dry. Serve hot, garnished with raisins, capers, and green olives, if desired.

Preparation time: 10 minutes
Cooking time: 35 to 40 minutes
Serves 4 to 6

*After handling raw chicken or other poultry, always remember to thoroughly wash your hands, utensils, and preparation area with soapy hot water. Also, when checking chicken for doneness, it's a good idea to cut it open gently to make sure that the meat is white (not pink) all the way through.

Cuban Meatloaf/ Salpicón

A spicy cousin of the standard meatloaf of the United States, this entrée is a favorite of diners young and old.

2 lb. lean ground beef

I egg

I small green bell pepper, seeded and chopped

I small yellow onion, chopped

4 cloves garlic, peeled and minced

½ c. seasoned bread crumbs

½ c. red wine vinegar

I tsp. paprika

¾ tsp. salt

¼ tsp. pepper

I c. creole sauce (recipe on page 40)

2 links chorizo

1. Preheat oven to 350°F.

2. In a large mixing bowl, combine beef, egg, green pepper, onion, garlic, bread crumbs, vinegar, paprika, salt, pepper, and half of the creole sauce. Mix well, using your hands if necessary, until all ingredients are thoroughly blended.

3. Spread half the meat mixture in a 9 x 5-inch loaf pan. Place the two links of sausage side by side on top of the meat mixture and cover with remaining meat mixture.

4. Pour the remaining creole sauce over the loaf. Cover with foil and bake for 1 hour. Remove foil and bake 15 minutes more, or until loaf is well browned and starting to pull away from the sides of the pan. Serve hot, with extra creole sauce if desired. If you like, turn the loaf out of the pan onto a platter to serve. If you do this, be sure to use oven mitts or have someone help you.

Preparation time: 20 to 25 minutes
Baking time: 1 hour 15 minutes
Serves 6

Beef Hash / *Picadillo*

Filling, flavorful picadillo is easy to prepare and makes a good winter meal. Like so many Cuban dishes, it is delicious with Cuban white rice (recipe on page 41).

1 tbsp. olive oil

1 green bell pepper, seeded and chopped

1 medium yellow onion, chopped

1 lb. lean ground beef*

½ c. creole sauce (recipe on page 40)

¼ tsp. cumin

salt and black pepper to taste

¼ c. sliced green olives with pimientos (optional)

¼ c. golden raisins (optional)

1. In a large, deep skillet or saucepan, heat oil over medium heat. Add green pepper and onion and sauté for 2 to 3 minutes, or until onion is soft but not brown.

2. Add ground beef. Use a spoon or spatula to break apart the beef and mix the ingredients together. Add creole sauce and cumin and stir well to mix.

3. Reduce heat and cover pan. Simmer slowly for about 30 minutes. Add salt and pepper to taste and serve hot. If desired, garnish with green olives and golden raisins.

Preparation time: 10 to 15 minutes
Cooking time: 35 to 40 minutes
Serves 4 to 6

*Want to create a fantastic vegetarian picadillo? Simply add 3 c. cubed, raw potatoes in Step 2 instead of the beef. Cook 20 minutes, or until potatoes are tender. This vegetarian dish is called picadillo a la criolla, or "creole hash."

Baked Eggs/Huevos al Plato

Many Cubans like to eat eggs for breakfast, but this dish also makes a wonderful lunch. Many diners have a slice of Cuban toast with their eggs. Cuban toast is made with crusty bread, similar to French or Italian bread, and eaten with butter or olive oil.

¼ c. olive oil

3 cloves garlic, peeled and minced

1 large onion, chopped

1 large green bell pepper, seeded and chopped

1 large tomato, chopped, or 8 oz. canned diced tomatoes

salt and pepper to taste

6 eggs

3 tbsp. butter, melted

1. Preheat oven to 350°F.

2. In a large, deep skillet, heat oil over medium heat. Sauté garlic, onion, and green pepper for 2 to 3 minutes, or until onion is soft but not brown. Add tomato and cook 15 minutes, or until sauce thickens. Add salt and pepper to taste.

3. Lightly oil six ramekins. Divide sauce evenly among ramekins. Break 1 egg into each dish, being careful not to break the yolk.* Drizzle a bit of melted butter over each egg.

4. Place dishes in oven and bake for 10 to 12 minutes, or until the whites of the eggs are completely opaque and white, and the yolks are still a bit runny. Remove from oven, season with additional salt and pepper if desired, and serve immediately.

*To make this step easier, try cracking each egg onto a saucer or small plate and sliding it gently into the ramekin.

Preparation time: 20 minutes
Cooking and baking time: 35 to 40 minutes
Serves 6

Desserts

In a country that abounds with fresh fruit, it's not surprising that many Cuban meals end with a fruit course, from pineapple rings and wedges of mango to slices of juicy guava and melon. But Cubans also love rich desserts, and cooks on the island prepare a wide range of delicious treats to satisfy any diner's sweet tooth.

Some favorite Cuban desserts have Spanish origins, including rice pudding and the classic baked custard known as flan. Sweet baked plantains, on the other hand, offer a taste of Cubans' African heritage. Other desserts take advantage of native ingredients, such as the tropical fruit in sweet *batidos de leche* (milk shakes).

Cuban desserts are delightfully sweet. Mango and papaya milk shake (left, recipe on page 59), rice pudding (right, recipe on page 58), and baked custard (bottom, recipe on pages 60–61) feature an array of tastes and textures.

Rice Pudding / Arroz con Leche

This sweet rice dish is well worth the time it takes to prepare. You can serve it warm or refrigerate it and serve it chilled.

1½ c. short-grain rice*

3 c. water

pinch of salt

1 cinnamon stick

grated peel of 1 lime**

8 c. milk

1 tsp. vanilla extract

1¼ c. sugar

ground cinnamon

*Many Cuban cooks use Valencia rice, a short-grain variety from Spain. If you can't find Valencia rice, you can use Arborio rice or other short-grain rice.

**Use a potato peeler or zester to gently remove peel in small strips from the lime. Try to avoid getting the white pith, which has a bitter taste. Chop or mince the peel with a knife for even smaller pieces.

1. Use a strainer to rinse rice in cold water until water runs almost clear. Place rice, water, and salt in a large saucepan and bring to a boil over high heat. Reduce heat, cover, and simmer 20 minutes, or until water is gone and rice is tender.

2. Add cinnamon stick and grated lime peel. Keeping pan over low heat, add milk 1 c. at a time, stirring constantly. After half the milk has been added, stir in vanilla, then add the remaining 4 c. milk, 1 c. at a time.

3. Continue stirring frequently for about 1 hour, or until all the milk has been absorbed and rice is creamy. Gradually stir in sugar and cook 5 to 7 minutes longer over low heat. Remove cinnamon stick. Dish pudding into eight small bowls and dust with cinnamon.

Preparation time: 5 minutes
Cooking time: 1 to 1½ hours
Serves 8

Mango and Papaya Milk Shake/
Batido de Mango y Papaya

This refreshing tropical fruit drink can be a healthy and satisfying end to a meal. Depending on how sweet you like your batido, you may choose to add more or less sugar.

1 c. diced mango, fresh or canned*

1 c. diced papaya, fresh or canned*

1 to 2 tbsp. sugar

1 c. cold milk

⅔ c. crushed ice

1. Place all ingredients in a blender. Puree until smooth and frosty.

2. Pour into tall glasses and serve immediately.

Preparation time: 10 minutes
Serves 3 to 4

*If you use fresh fruit, prepare the mango by carefully cutting lengthwise slits through the skin of the mango. Tear skin away from the fruit in strips until all the peel is removed. Cut the flesh, removing the large flat seed in the center of the fruit. To prepare papaya, use a vegetable peeler to remove the skin. Cut fruit in half lengthwise, and use a spoon to scoop out the small black seeds and the stringy fruit. Dice flesh.

Baked Custard/*Flan*

This rich, sweet dish, introduced to local cooks by the Spanish, remains a favorite throughout Cuba and other Latin American countries.

4 eggs

14-oz. can sweetened condensed milk

1½ c. evaporated milk

1 tsp. vanilla extract

2 tbsp. plus 1½ c. sugar

1. Preheat oven to 350°F.

2. In a large mixing bowl, beat the eggs lightly. Add sweetened condensed milk, evaporated milk, vanilla, and 2 tbsp. sugar. Stir well.

3. Place remaining sugar in a heavy saucepan over medium heat. When sugar is heated, it turns into a caramel-colored liquid, referred to as caramelized sugar. Cook sugar for 8 to 10 minutes, or until completely melted, stirring constantly so that it doesn't burn. When the melted sugar begins to bubble, remove from heat and continue stirring until it stops bubbling. Don't touch or taste the caramelized sugar, as it is extremely hot and sticky.

4. Carefully but quickly pour caramelized sugar into molds* and swirl gently to coat the sides.

5. Carefully pour egg mixture into sugar-coated molds.

6. Place molds into a larger pan or shallow baking dish. Pour about ¼ inch of water into the pan or dish. Place in oven and bake for 40 to 45 minutes, or until flan is set. When done, a knife or toothpick inserted into the center of the flan should come out nearly clean. Be careful not to overbake, as the flan will have a tough consistency.

7. Remove molds from oven and cool on a wire rack before transferring to refrigerator. Chill at least 1 hour. To serve, carefully run a knife along the edge of each mold and tip flan out, upside-down, onto dessert plates. The caramelized sugar inside the molds will run down over the top of each serving of flan.

Preparation time: 20 minutes
(plus 1½ hours cooling time)
Baking time: 40 to 45 minutes
Serves 6

*You can use six 6-oz. ramekins or custard cups for flan molds. You can also use one 9-in. pie pan. If you use the pan, you may need to bake flan for an hour or more.

Holiday and Festival Food

Through good times and bad, Cuban families and friends try to be together for special occasions. Usually, the festivities include at least one or two special dishes. Pork is one of the most popular holiday foods, and lechón asado (roast suckling pig) shows up at celebrations from Christmas to Carnaval. Many cooks prepare their lechón asado according to recipes that have been passed down through generations. A Cuban pig roast is usually a grand production, which may include setting up a fire pit in the backyard.

Because of the restrictions on religious observances in the past, many festive foods are not strongly associated with specific Cuban holidays. Instead these foods are connected with good times and celebration in general. Prepare the dishes in this section anytime to turn an ordinary meal into a special event and to celebrate the Cuban way.

Serve fried yucca with garlic sauce (bottom, recipe on page 65) or red beans and rice (top, recipe on pages 66–67) on Christmas Eve or anytime you want to feel festive.

Roast Pork/ *Cerdo Asado*

This recipe is easier to make than a traditional roast pig, but it still gives you a taste of roast pork, Cuban style.

Marinade:

4 cloves garlic, peeled

¼ tsp. oregano

¼ tsp. salt

¼ tsp. black pepper

½ c. sour orange juice*

2 lb. boneless pork tenderloin, trimmed

*You may be able to find sour orange juice in Latin American markets or specialty grocery stores. Otherwise, in this recipe you can replace it with a mixture of ¼ c. regular orange juice, 2 tbsp. fresh lime juice, and 2 tbsp. fresh lemon juice.

1. Mash garlic cloves, using a mortar and pestle, or a small bowl and a fork, or the back of a spoon. To make marinade, combine mashed garlic, oregano, salt, pepper, and sour orange juice in a large bowl. Set aside 2 tbsp. of the marinade in the refrigerator.

2. Place pork in marinade and use your hands to coat meat well with marinade. Cover and refrigerate 3 to 4 hours.

3. Preheat oven to 325°F. Remove pork from marinade and place in a baking dish. Discard all but reserved 2 tbsp. of marinade.

4. Place pork in oven. Roast pork, uncovered, for 1½ hours, or until a meat thermometer inserted into the center of roast reads 155°F to 165°F. If meat looks dry during roasting, baste with a small amount of reserved marinade. Let roast cool for 10 minutes before slicing to serve.

Preparation time: 10 minutes
(plus 3 to 4 hours marinating time)
Cooking time: 1½ hours
Serves 6 to 8

Fried Yucca with Garlic Sauce/
Yuca Frita con Mojo

Fried yucca, smothered in a zesty garlic sauce, makes a perfect side dish for roast pork.

Garlic sauce (mojo):

6 cloves garlic, peeled

1 tsp. salt

½ c. sour orange juice*

1 large white onion, very thinly sliced

Fried yucca:

1½ lb. yucca (frozen yucca may be available in Latin markets)**

1 tsp. salt

⅓ c. olive or vegetable oil

See note on page 64 for a substitution for sour orange juice.

**If you can't find yucca, you can make this dish with potatoes instead. The flavor and texture won't be quite the same, but the tangy sauce will give you a taste of what true Cuban yucca frita con mojo is like.*

1. To make the mojo, use a food processor or mortar and pestle to crush garlic cloves and salt into a thick paste. In a mixing bowl, combine garlic paste, sour orange juice, and onion. Mix well and let sit at room temperature for at least 30 minutes.

2. While mojo sits, peel yucca and cut into 2-inch sticks. Place in a saucepan with salt and just enough water to cover. Bring to a boil. Reduce heat, cover, and simmer for 30 minutes, or until tender. Remove pan from heat and drain. Be sure to remove any tough parts from the center of the yucca. Leave yucca sticks in saucepan.

3. In another saucepan, combine mojo and oil. Cook over medium-high heat until bubbling. Remove from heat and transfer to saucepan with yucca. Toss lightly and sauté over medium heat until barely browned. Serve hot.

Preparation time: 20 to 30 minutes
Cooking time: 45 to 50 minutes
Serves 4 to 6

Red Beans and Rice/ *Congrí*

Although black beans are eaten more commonly than red beans in most of Cuba, people who live on the eastern tip of the island prefer red beans. This classic rice and bean dish is an old favorite for Christmas Eve.

1 c. dried small red kidney beans*

8 c. water

½ small onion

1 small red or green bell pepper (seeded and chopped except for one strip, left whole)

2 fresh cilantro sprigs

½ tsp. plus ½ tsp. cumin

4 cloves garlic (2 cloves peeled and left whole, and 2 minced)

salt and pepper to taste

1½ c. long-grain white rice

3 tbsp. olive oil

2 medium yellow onions, chopped

½ tsp. oregano

1. Place beans in a large bowl with enough cold water to cover by 3 inches. Allow to soak for at least 4 hours or overnight.

2. Drain beans and place in a large pot with 8 c. water, onion half, strip of bell pepper, cilantro, ½ tsp. cumin, and 2 whole garlic cloves. Bring to a boil over medium-high heat. Reduce heat to medium and cover pot. Simmer for about 50 minutes, stirring occasionally, until beans are tender. Season to taste with salt and pepper.

3. Drain beans, saving cooking liquid. Remove onion, bell pepper, cilantro, and garlic from pot and discard.

4. Use a strainer to rinse rice in cold water until water runs almost clear. Place 3 c. of the bean-cooking liquid in a heavy saucepan and bring to a boil. Add rice and return to a boil. Reduce heat to medium-low, cover, and simmer 20 minutes, or until almost all the liquid is absorbed. Remove pan from heat, and fluff rice with a fork.

5. In a large, deep skillet, heat oil over medium-high heat. Add chopped onions, chopped bell pepper, minced garlic, remaining cumin, and oregano. Sauté 5 minutes, or until onions are soft and just beginning to brown. Stir in beans and rice, and cook until heated through. Add salt and pepper to taste, and serve hot.

Preparation time: 20 minutes
(plus 4 hours soaking time)
Cooking time: 1½ to 1¾ hours
Serves 4 to 6

* If you like, you can replace dried beans with 15 oz. canned beans. Skip Step 1, and simmer for just 25 minutes in Step 2.

Cuban Cookies / *Torticas*

These sugar cookies flavored with tart lime juice are delightfully zippy. Longtime favorites of Cuban children, they make special treats for birthdays and other celebrations.

¼ lb. (1 stick) butter, at room temperature

1 c. sugar

2 egg yolks*

1 tsp. fresh lime juice

½ tsp. grated lime peel**

1 tsp. vanilla extract

1½ c. all-purpose flour

½ tsp. salt

1 tsp. baking powder

powdered sugar for sprinkling

1. In a large bowl, cream butter and sugar with an electric mixer or a wooden spoon.

2. Add egg yolks, lime juice, lime peel, and vanilla. Blend thoroughly.

3. Mix flour, salt, and baking powder in a separate bowl. Add to butter mixture and mix well. Wrap dough in waxed paper and refrigerate for 1 hour.

4. Preheat oven to 375°F. Use your fingers to form dough into walnut-sized balls and place on an ungreased baking sheet. Bake 8 to 10 minutes, or until very lightly browned. Allow cookies to cool on baking sheet for 5 minutes before removing to a wire rack and sprinkling with powdered sugar.

Preparation time: 20 minutes
(plus 1 hour refrigeration)
Baking time: 8 to 10 minutes
Makes 3 to 4 dozen cookies

*To separate an egg, crack it cleanly on the edge of a nonplastic bowl. Holding the two halves of the eggshell over the bowl, gently pour the egg yolk back and forth between the two halves. Let the egg white fall into the bowl and be careful not to break the yolk. When most of the egg white has been separated, drop yolk into a second bowl.

**See note on page 58 for a tip on how to grate lime peel.

Index

About the Authors

Alison Behnke is an author and editor of children's books. She also enjoys traveling and experiencing new cultures and cuisines. Among her other books are *Cooking the Brazilian Way*, *Vegetarian Cooking around the World*, *Italy in Pictures*, *Japan in Pictures*, and *Afghanistan in Pictures*.

Victor Manuel Valens was born in Havana, Cuba, in 1950. In 1961 his family moved to New York City, where his father worked as a chef. From an early age, Victor was "Dad's prep boy" and learned how to cook Cuban food by helping him prepare meals. Victor and his wife, Niki, a native of Cyprus, own a restaurant in Minneapolis called Victor's 1959 Café, where they serve authentic Cuban home cooking.

Photo Acknowledgments
The photographs in this book are reproduced courtesy of: © Marco Cristofori/CORBIS, pp. 2–3; © Walter & Louiseann Pietrowicz/September 8th Stock, pp. 4, 5, 6, 18, 30, 33, 37, 38, 43, 48, 53, 56, 62, 69; © Robert van der Hilst/CORBIS, p. 11; © Dewitt Jones/CORBIS, p. 12; © Daniel Lainé/CORBIS, pp. 15, 16; © Amos Nachoum/CORBIS, p. 26.

Cover photos and spine: © Walter & Louiseann Pietrowicz/September 8th Stock, all.

The illustrations on pages 7, 19, 27, 31, 32, 34, 35, 36, 39, 40, 42, 45, 47, 49, 50, 51, 54, 55, 57, 58, 59, 61, 63, 64, 65, 67, and 68 are by Tim Seeley.
The map on page 8 is by Bill Hauser.